Unlocking Business Potential: Possibilities and Opportunities for Entrepreneurs and SMEs

Dr.P. Koshy

Author|Entrepreneur|Development Professional. Writes on #SMEs, #Entrepreneurship. Director at TdwMedia; IERD- Enterprise Institute; Editor The World of Startups, Global SME News: Former Senior Economist at World Association for SMEs/ Former Economist AMI International SAOC;
Studied at Mumbai University, NMIMS University , Mumbai and KC College, Mumbai. Email.<caushie@gmail.com>;
Linkedin: https://www.linkedin.com/in/caushie

17 July 2023
Webinar Presentation
Organized by
INSEEDS, ADORE, and SIMTRAK

Unlocking Business Potential: Possibilities and Opportunities for Entrepreneurs and SMEs

Dr.P. Koshy

TDW Productions & Publishing

*Unlocking Business Potential: Possibilities
and Opportunities for
Entrepreneurs and SMEs*

P. Koshy

*First published in India by TDW
All Rights Reserved.
©2023
Published by
TDW Productions & Publishing*

*Type Setting & Design
TDW Digital Graphics
thedigitalwordhub@gmail.com
Web: www. http://tdwpublishing.com*

Unlocking Business Potential: Possibilities and Opportunities for Entrepreneurs and SMEs

Empowering Entrepreneurs and SMEs: Digital Transformation , and Sustainable Development

Contents

Unlocking Business Potential

- Business potential
- Entrepreneurs
- SMEs
- Opportunities
- Youth entrepreneurs
- Economic growth
- Innovation
- Job creation
- Dynamic business landscape
- Challenges
- Digital transformation
- Industry 4.0
- AI
- Recession

Economic Reforms

- Entrepreneurial culture
- British Raj
- License and Permit Raj
- New Industrial Policy
- Deregulations
- School days in Kerala
- Entrepreneurship development

- Digital infrastructure
- Market opportunities

Ease of Doing Business

- Simplified Business Registration
- Single Window Clearance
- Tax Reforms
- Insolvency and Bankruptcy Code (IBC)
- Labour Reforms
- Digital Initiatives
- Infrastructure Development
- Investor Protection
- Compliance burden
- Economic growth

Framework to Understand Emerging Business Opportunities

- Sustainable Development Goals (SDGs)
- Renewable Energy Industry
- Sustainable Agriculture
- Responsible Tourism
- Circular Economy
- Education and Skill Development
- Sustainability
- Social, economic, and environmental objectives
- Responsible consumption
- Value-added product development

Digital Economy, Gig Workers, Sharing Economy, Industry 4.0

- Fourth Industrial Revolution
- Digital Transformation
- Innovation and Agility
- Collaboration and Networking
- Talent Development and Upskilling
- Cybersecurity
- Data Privacy
- Access to Finance
- Financial inclusion
- Market Linkages
- Agro-tech-smart farming

Focus: Key Sectors and Markets

- Youth entrepreneurs
- E-commerce platforms
- Digital Marketing
- Export Promotion
- Financial sector services
- Technology adoption
- Solar installation
- Traditional artisan businesses
- Handicrafts
- Digital identity
- Market access

Agenda of Doubling Farmer Income (DFI)

- Dairy cooperatives
- Agricultural Technology and Services
- Value Chain Enhancement
- Market Linkages

- Financial Inclusion
- Capacity Building
- Skill Development
- Post-harvest management
- Precision farming
- Microfinance
- Crop insurance

Social Media Marketing, Platforms and digital marketing

- HAM SHILPAKAR
- Artisans Network
- Indian handloom and handicraft sector
- Digital identity
- Market access
- Environmentally friendly products
- Social media-based platform
- Handmade products
- Cultural heritage
- Artisan community

Opportunities for youth entrepreneurs

- E-commerce platforms
- Rural agro-businesses
- Agro-tech-smart farming
- Solar installation and maintenance
- Exporting products
- Facilitating exports
- Digital marketing
- Business support services
- Financial sector services
- Business plan
- Market data
- Market research

Project Progress Challenge: Elevate Your Entreprenuria Skills

- Intervention
- Business establishment
- Identifying farmers
- Strategies
- Handicrafts
- Traditional artisan businesses
- Business plan preparation
- Research
- Business plan formulation

References

Annex:

1. Unlocking Farmer Prosperity: Strategies for Multiplying Income and Strengthening Market Linkages

2. Khadi: the new corporate attire?

Unlocking Business Potential: Possibilities and Opportunities for Entrepreneurs and SMEs

It's an honor to be part of this web meeting/webinar today. Before I begin, I would like to extend my heartfelt congratulations to the organizers – INSEEDS, ADORE, and SIMTRAK. Their tireless dedication has brought together a diverse assembly of young, vibrant minds.

Today's webinar revolves around a theme that resonates deeply in the current dynamic business landscape - "Unlocking Business Potential: Possibilities and Opportunities for Entrepreneurs and SMEs." This theme is not just a collection of words; it's a beacon illuminating the path to economic growth, innovation, and job creation, with the ambitious torchbearers being our youth entrepreneurs.

Technological transformations at various levels

The world of business is undergoing a transformation of epic proportions, a symphony of change that plays both daunting challenges and harmonious opportunities. In these times, forums like the one we're in become not just valuable but invaluable.

The air is also thick with concerns - talk of looming economic recession, the ever-encroaching fear of AI, generative AI, and the sweeping tide of digital transformation that threatens employment opportunities, leaving people to wonder about the future of the human touch in business. However, it's crucial to acknowledge that these fears often find little footing in reality. In today's landscape of AI and Industry 4.0 technologies, it's crucial to recognize that these advancements need not kill jobs; instead, they have the potential to create even more employment opportunities.

INSEEDS, our esteemed host, has consistently demonstrated exceptional dedication to nurturing opportunities and development for individuals from diverse backgrounds. Their unwavering commitment to creating spaces for collaboration, learning, and inspiration is nothing short of commendable. It is through endeavors like this webinar that we collectively embark on the journey to empower and uplift entrepreneurs and SMEs. These are the backbone of our economy, poised to unlock their true potential and leave an indelible mark in their respective industries.

Indian economy, reforms: Transforming India's Business Landscape

India boasts a rich entrepreneurial heritage deeply entrenched in its cottage industries, traditional village enterprises, and the agricultural sector. Regrettably, during the colonial era under British rule, our entrepreneurial roots were severely weakened.

However, the clarion call for independence galvanized a reinvigorated focus on reinvigorating our rural economy and nurturing entrepreneurship, symbolized by the iconic Charkha (spinning wheel) and the principle of self-reliance.

In the post-independence period, our economic policies predominantly centered on public sector undertakings, entailing stringent governmental oversight and an overwhelming regulatory framework. This period, an era of "License and Permit Raj", called by Rajaji, was marked by exhaustive inspections and the prerequisite of licenses and permits for almost every facet of business operations.

License Raj

The term "License Raj," coined by Chakravarti Rajagopalachari, describes a system where the Indian government had a lot of control and regulations over the economy from the 1950s to the early 1990s. Under this system, businesses needed government licenses to operate, and getting these licenses was often a difficult and complicated process.

Within this framework, Indian businesses were obligated to secure government licenses to conduct their operations, and the acquisition of these licenses was often a challenging and arduous process.

It required private companies to satisfy numerous government agencies—sometimes up to 80—before they could start producing things. Even after getting a license, the government continued to regulate production.

Rajagopalachari believed that the License Raj could lead to political corruption and economic stagnation. He was so concerned about this that he founded the Swatantra Party to oppose these practices.He believed in encouraging competition and protecting workers' rights while also limiting the role of government in certain industries. He opposed government interference in trade and the bureaucracy that came with it.

In a nutshell, the License Raj was a system of heavy government control over the economy, with many regulations and approvals needed to do business. This system, despite its intentions, hindered economic growth and created inefficiencies.Nonetheless, a significant transformation unfolded in 1991 with the introduction of the New Industrial Policy and subsequent deregulation initiatives that realigned our economic policy framework.

Economic reforms of 1991 created new opportunities

The economic reforms of 1991 in India heralded a new era of opportunity for the country's youth. These reforms, characterized by liberalization, privatization, and globalization, brought about significant positive changes.

With the opening up of various sectors and the expansion of industries, job creation soared, offering a plethora of employment options to the young workforce. Simultaneously, entrepreneurship flourished, as the reforms simplified business establishment and management, providing a platform for innovative young minds to explore their ideas.

The surge in economic activity also boosted the demand for higher education and vocational training, equipping the youth with the skills needed for better job prospects. Moreover, the global exposure resulting from globalization empowered Indian youth to compete on a worldwide scale, fostering a spirit of innovation and competitiveness.

With economic growth came increased incomes, enabling young people to enhance their living standards and save for the future. Rapid urbanization, driven by economic growth, led to the creation of urban centers with better infrastructure, drawing youth seeking improved living conditions and job opportunities. Furthermore, the reforms expanded the financial sector, promoting greater financial inclusion and providing the youth with better access to banking and financial services, thereby broadening their economic horizons.

Reflecting on my school days in Kerala up until the 1990s, one scarcely encountered the term "entrepreneur," and job prospects were limited, with few avenues of specialization and meager opportunities in the private sector. Today, the landscape has undergone a profound metamorphosis. Entrepreneurship development cells and courses have proliferated across educational institutions throughout the nation.

The complexities of brand establishment and marketing, once formidable and cost-intensive, have now become significantly more accessible. In contemporary times, initiating a business venture has become markedly more straightforward, with a streamlined process that experts and international agencies and our own experience prove that its 80% faster. An array of digital tools and infrastructure is available virtually cost-free.

Furthermore, India's expansive market offers a multitude of opportunities for entrepreneurs and small and medium-sized enterprises (SMEs). From agriculturists and artisans to cottage industries and SMEs, the business arena and marketplace beckon for exploration and expansion.

These monumental changes transcend mere reforms; they signify a revolution reshaping the narrative of India's business landscape. The new India is of opportunities. It's the coming back and revival in full strength India's entrepreneurial legacy.

In the early 1990s, India confronted a significant economic crisis marked by a foreign exchange deficit, precipitating a pronounced economic downturn. In response to this predicament, the government initiated a series of economic adjustments through a package of reforms known as 'structural reforms' under the rubric of the 'New Economic Policy (NEP).'

The New Economic Policy initiatives encompasses a suite of governmental economic activities and encompasses various policy instruments aimed at bolstering macroeconomic stability. These measures encompass stabilisation actions designed to curb inflation and rectify the Balance of Payments (BoP) weaknesses, as well as structural reform measures intended to enhance economic efficiency and heighten international competitiveness. The macro economic stabilisation program encompass initiatives pursued by the government to:

- Restrain inflation by keeping the prices of goods in check.
- Maintain an adequate foreign exchange reserve to address BoP vulnerabilities.
- In conjunction with these stabilisation measures, the government also launched Structural Reform Measures, representing long-term initiatives geared towards:
- Enhancing the overall efficiency of the economy.
- Alleviating rigidity in various segments of the Indian economy to boost international competitiveness.

The objectives of the New Economic Policy, 1991, were multi-faceted:

- To integrate the Indian economy into the global arena, charting a new course for the Indian market.
- To mitigate inflation rates and accumulate foreign exchange reserves, thereby accelerating economic growth.
- To increase private sector participation in economic growth by reducing government-controlled sectors.
- To facilitate the global flow of goods, services, capital, human resources, and technology by reducing trade constraints.
- To attain economic stability and create an unencumbered economic market by eliminating superfluous trade and tariff restrictions.

The components of the New Economic Policy, 1991, revolve around three pivotal concepts: Liberalisation, Privatisation, and Globalisation. This model supplanted the earlier Licence Raj . The prime goal of these reforms was to stimulate rapid economic growth, lower inflation rates, reduce fiscal deficits, and rectify the BoP crisis.

Liberalisation is a cornerstone of the NEP, signaling a shift from government control to a more open and market-driven economic system. Prior to 1991, the government held sway over the private sector, hampering decision-making within domestic industries. The liberalisation policy sought to empower these sectors with greater autonomy, eliminating government interference.

The government's abolition of the licensing system was instrumental in streamlining industrial activities, reducing bureaucratic delays and corruption. Under the Liberalisation Policy, various economic reforms were introduced, including those in the industrial sector, financial sector, tax regime, foreign exchange, and trade and investment policies.

Privatisation involves the transfer of ownership and operation of public sector enterprises to the private sector. This transition was necessitated by the underperformance of public sector undertakings, which resulted in poor product quality and services for consumers. Privatisation promotes diversification, higher profits, customer satisfaction, productivity, and growth, all within a competitive environment.

Globalisation is the integration of the Indian economy with the global arena, fostering the free flow of trade, capital, information, technology, and people. This policy aimed to enhance economic development by facilitating collaboration with multinational corporations, reducing trade barriers, promoting exports, and attracting foreign investments.

The measures instituted under the LPG Policy included opening the market to foreign investments and international trade,
reducing reliance on foreign loans, expanding the banking and
capital sectors, increasing competition through privatisation,
and improving the quality of goods and services. Globalisation,
in turn, connected the local market with the global economy,
attracted foreign direct investments, and reduced international
trade restrictions, ultimately enhancing India's position in the
global financial markets.

Unlocking Opportunities for Young Entrepreneurs

To shed light on the abundant entrepreneurial prospects available, let me present a case study featuring Leela.

Case of Leela:
Leela, a widowed entrepreneur hailing from Kerala, shoulders
the responsibility of providing for her family, which includes
three children. One is a college student, while the other two face
unemployment due to disabilities. Together, they have embarked
on a journey into the realm of organic farming with a particular
focus on dairy production. Leela manages a farm comprising
four dairy cows and predominantly sustains her livelihood by
marketing milk and dairy products.

An astute and resourceful entrepreneur, Leela capitalizes on
the copious grass supply found in the neighboring uncultivated
paddy fields in Kottayam, Kerala. By doing so, she curbs her
reliance on costly cattle feed, leading to substantial cost savings
while elevating the distinctive qualities of her milk and dairy
produce.

Particularly noteworthy is the organic grass-fed ghee crafted
by Leela, renowned for its exquisite flavor and aroma, especial-

ly among Non-Resident Indians (NRIs). Astonishingly, Leela remains oblivious to the exceptional qualities of her grass-fed cow's ghee.

In contrast to the market price for organic grass-fed cow's ghee on e-commerce platforms such as "Amazon India" and Flipkart, which often falls within the range of INR 950 to INR 1000 for 500 grams, Leela sells her ghee locally at a significantly reduced rate of INR 300 for the same quantity. However, she grapples with the challenge of securing equitable prices for her products and expanding her market reach.

Leela's story is emblematic of countless farmers seeking fair remuneration for their produce. Herein lies an opportunity: fostering their integration into global value chains, facilitating their entry into e-commerce platforms, or even venturing into product exports.

There exists a pressing need to nurture Indian local brands and elevate them to global recognition. By fostering the development of Indian SME brands with a formidable global footprint, our focus rests on digital marketing and the implementation of effective communication strategies to engage diverse international audiences.

The revival of Khadi, the hand-woven fabric, presents an environmentally conscious paradigm by embracing eco-friendly techniques and sustainable practices. It embodies a responsible approach to manufacturing and aligns with the growing global demand for eco-friendly products.

Encouraging the Khadi movement and endorsing Khadi-made suits and dresses as the Corporate Dress Code could serve as a meaningful campaign.As part of our commitment to empowering rural communities and farmers, active support for Farmer Producer Organizations (FPOs) and farmer groups becomes paramount. By equipping them with essential resources, imparting training, and enabling market access, we not only bolster their livelihoods but also champion locally sourced, sustainable merchandise. This endeavor contributes to the holistic development of the agricultural sector while uplifting the rural economy.

Streamlining Business Setup

Several reform measures, initiated paved the Way for Effortless Business Establishment. Setting up a business today is 80% quicker and smoother, observed Dr. Rajan Sudesh Ratna, Senior Economic Affairs Officer at UN ESCAP, who was speaking at a meeting organized by ISED.

According to Economist Intelligence Unit's, BUSINES EN-VORNMENT India ranks 10th as per its latest ranking for 2023. the report noted that ". Policy reforms are making it easier to do business in India, and we expect major improvements in areas such as infrastructure, taxation, and trade regulation, boosting investment," Sound digital infrastructure, and favourable demographics, improvements in the country's business environment are reducing the risks

 India has implemented significant reforms to improve the ease of doing business in the country. These reforms are aimed at creating a business-friendly environment, attracting investments, and promoting entrepreneurship. Here are some key areas where reforms have been implemented:

•	Simplified Business Registration: India has simplified the process of starting a business by introducing online registration platforms. Entrepreneurs can now register their businesses more easily and quickly, reducing bureaucratic hurdles.
•	Single Window Clearance: The introduction of single

window clearance systems streamlines the process of obtaining various licenses and permits. This centralized platform allows businesses to submit applications and receive clearances from multiple government departments, saving time and reducing administrative burden.

•	Tax Reforms: The Goods and Services Tax (GST) has replaced multiple indirect taxes, unifying the tax structure across the country. This has simplified the tax compliance process for businesses and reduced the complexity of doing business in different states.

•	Insolvency and Bankruptcy Code (IBC): The IBC has strengthened the legal framework for resolving insolvency cases, providing a more efficient and time-bound process for debt recovery. This has increased investor confidence and improved the ease of exiting businesses.

•	Labour Reforms: Labour laws have been rationalized to provide flexibility to businesses while protecting workers' rights. The introduction of labor codes has simplified and consolidated various labor laws, promoting ease of compliance for businesses.

•	Digital Initiatives: India has embraced digitalization in various sectors, including business registration, tax filings, and compliance procedures. Online platforms and digital services have made it easier for businesses to interact with government departments and complete necessary procedures remotely.

•	Infrastructure Development: focusing improvement in physical infrastructure, such as roads, ports, and logistics networks, which enhances connectivity, reduces transportation costs, and facilitates the movement of goods and services across the country.

•	Investor Protection: Measures have been taken to strengthen investor protection and corporate governance norms. This includes greater transparency, disclosure requirements, and enhanced mechanisms for resolving shareholder disputes.

•	These ease of doing business reforms in India have resulted in significant improvements in the World Bank's Doing Business rankings. They have helped attract investments, foster entrepreneurship, and create a more conducive environment for businesses to thrive. The government continues to prioritize reforms to further enhance the ease of doing business in the country, promoting economic growth and development.

- Reduction in compliance burden:
- GOI (Central Ministries, states and Uts) have decriminalised more than 3,500 provisions related to minor technical or procedural defaults (Source: Economic Survey 2022-23)
- reduced more than 39,000 compliances to foster ease of doing business as of January 17, 2023, according to the Economic Survey 2022-23.'
- New technologies will further reduce compliance burden. Monitoring of transactions, payments, labour related aspects, Supply Chain monitoring
- India has emerged as one of the most attractive destinations not only for investments but also for doing business
- Authorized Economic Operator Scheme (world Customs Organization) reduce compliance burden in trade/international trade(Exports-Imports)

Framework to understand emerging business opportunities: key aspect to focus

It is important for specific industries and SMEs to align their operations, products, and services with the principles and targets of the SDGs.

The Sustainable Development Goals (SDGs) provide a comprehensive framework for future economic activities and model to be focussed upon. SDGs encompasses a wide range of social, economic, and environmental objectives.

Renewable Energy Industry: The renewable energy industry plays a crucial role in achieving SDG 7 (Affordable and Clean Energy). By investing in and promoting renewable energy sources such as solar, wind, and hydroelectric power, this industry contributes to reducing greenhouse gas emissions, improving energy access, and promoting sustainable energy practices.

Sustainable Agriculture and Food Industry: SDG 2 (Zero Hunger) and SDG 12 (Responsible Consumption and Production) are closely linked to the agriculture and food industry. SMEs in this sector can promote sustainable farming practices, reduce food waste, and support local and organic food production. Adopting sustainable supply chains and promoting fair trade can also contribute to SDG 8 (Decent Work and Economic Growth).

Responsible Tourism and Hospitality Industry: The tourism and hospitality industry has a significant impact on several SDGs, including SDG 8 (Decent Work and Economic Growth), SDG 11 (Sustainable Cities and Communities), and SDG 12 (Responsible Consumption and Production). SMEs in this sector can adopt sustainable practices, promote cultural preservation, support local communities, and minimize environmental impacts through responsible tourism initiatives.

Circular Economy and Waste Management Industry: SDG 12 (Responsible Consumption and Production) is directly related to the circular economy and waste management industry. SMEs can focus on reducing waste generation, recycling and reusing materials, and promoting sustainable consumption patterns. This industry contributes to resource efficiency, waste reduction, and mitigating environmental pollution.

Education and Skill Development Industry: SDG 4 (Quality Education) and SDG 8 (Decent Work and Economic Growth) are central to the education and skill development industry. SMEs in this sector can provide vocational training, promote lifelong learning opportunities, and support inclusive education.

By equipping individuals with skills for sustainable employment, they contribute to poverty reduction and economic empowerment.

It is important for specific industries and SMEs to align their operations, products, and services with the principles and targets of the SDGs. This can be achieved by integrating sustainability into business strategies, adopting responsible practices, promoting innovation, and collaborating with stakeholders to address sustainable development challenges. By doing so, these industries and SMEs can make significant contributions to the global efforts towards achieving the SDGs and creating a more sustainable future for all.

Digital economy, Gig workers, Sharing economy, platforms, Industry 4.0.

The Fourth Industrial Revolution, characterized by the fusion of digital, physical, and biological technologies, presents both challenges and opportunities for small and medium-sized enterprises (SMEs).

Digital Transformation: SMEs need to embrace digital transformation to stay competitive in the Fourth Industrial Revolution. This involves adopting digital technologies and tools such as cloud computing, data analytics, artificial intelligence, and the Internet of Things (IoT) to streamline operations, improve efficiency, and enhance customer experiences. Embracing e-commerce and online platforms can also help SMEs reach new markets and customers.

Innovation and Agility: The Fourth Industrial Revolution emphasizes the importance of innovation and agility. SMEs should foster a culture of innovation, encouraging employees to think creatively and adapt to rapid technological advancements. By embracing new ideas, experimenting with emerging technologies, and being open to change, SMEs can stay ahead of the curve and seize new business opportunities.

Collaboration and Networking: Collaboration and networking are crucial for SMEs to thrive in the Fourth Industrial Revolution. Joining industry networks, participating in innovation ecosystems, and collaborating with larger companies, research institutions, and startups can provide access to resources, knowledge, and partnerships that enhance competitiveness and promote growth.

Talent Development and Upskilling: The Fourth Industrial Revolution demands a skilled workforce proficient in emerging technologies. SMEs should invest in talent development and upskilling programs to equip employees with the necessary digital skills. This can be achieved through training initiatives, partnerships with educational institutions, and participation in government-led skill development programs.

Cybersecurity and Data Privacy: As SMEs embrace digital technologies, cybersecurity and data privacy become paramount. SMEs need to prioritize implementing robust cybersecurity measures to protect sensitive business and customer data. Understanding and complying with relevant data privacy regulations is also crucial to maintain trust with customers and partners.

Access to Finance and Funding: SMEs often face challenges in accessing finance for technological investments and innovation. Governments and financial institutions should provide adequate support and funding mechanisms tailored to the needs of SMEs in the Fourth Industrial Revolution. This can include initiatives such as grants, loans, venture capital, and crowdfunding platforms.

By embracing digital transformation, fostering innovation, collaborating, upskilling employees, prioritizing cybersecurity, and

ensuring access to finance, SMEs can leverage the Fourth Industrial Revolution to drive growth, enhance competitiveness, and
create sustainable business models. Embracing these opportunities can position SMEs as key drivers of economic development
and contribute to a prosperous and inclusive digital future.

Focus: Key sectors and markets

•	There are significant business opportunities for youth
entrepreneurs to contribute to and support the agriculture-farm
economy, small and micro enterprises, and rural economy in
terms of digital marketing, digital transformation, export promotion, and eCommerce facilitation:

In E Commerce: there are lot of opportunities. Huge market. 80
percent of E Commerce is still dominated by B2B transactions
and only 20 percent by B2C.

There is a huge potential to set up local, regaional and national level e commerce platforms focussing on B2C. The global
e-commerce market size is reached US$ 16.6 Trillion in 2022 and
its growing. According to a Deloitte India Report titled 'Future
of Retail,' India's online retail market size is expected to reach
US$ 325 billion by 2030, up from US$ 70 billion in 2022.

•	Digital Marketing for Agriculture and Rural Products:
Youth entrepreneurs can utilize digital marketing strategies
to promote and market agricultural products, locally sourced
goods, and handicrafts from rural areas. By creating engaging
online content, leveraging social media platforms, and implementing targeted marketing campaigns, they can connect farmers and rural entrepreneurs with a wider consumer base, both
domestically and internationally.
•	Digital Transformation in Agriculture and Rural Busi-
nesses: Implementing digital technologies and tools in agricultur-

al practices and rural businesses can drive efficiency, productivity, and innovation. Youth entrepreneurs can develop solutions such as farm management software, IoT-enabled devices for smart agriculture, and supply chain optimization platforms. By helping farmers and rural enterprises adopt these technologies, they can enable them to streamline operations, reduce costs, and enhance overall sustainability.

•	Export Promotion for Rural Products: Youth entrepreneurs can play a crucial role in facilitating the export of rural products to international markets. They can establish export networks, provide market research and intelligence, and assist in obtaining necessary certifications and compliance requirements. By bridging the gap between rural producers and global buyers, they can unlock new market opportunities and generate economic growth for rural communities.

•	eCommerce Facilitation for Rural Entrepreneurs: Building on the growing eCommerce trend, youth entrepreneurs can support rural entrepreneurs and small-scale businesses in establishing an online presence and selling their products through eCommerce platforms. This includes assisting with website development, online store setup, logistics, and payment gateways. By embracing eCommerce, rural entrepreneurs can access a wider customer base and overcome geographical limitations.

•	youth entrepreneurs have a unique opportunity to contribute to the agriculture-farm economy, small and micro enterprises, and the rural economy through digital marketing, digital transformation, export promotion, and eCommerce facilitation. By harnessing these avenues, they can drive economic growth, empower rural communities, and promote sustainability in these sectors.

Opportunities in farm sector, Agr-based enterprises, AGENDA OF DOUBLING FARMER INCOME (DFI)

- Agenda of doubling farmer income (DFI) presents a significant opportunity for entrepreneurs to support farmer communities and farmer organizations.
- Dairy cooperatives in India there are close to 30 dairy Milk Cooperative Federations and close to two lakh primary dairy societies and around 2 lakh primary milk societies.
- Plans to expand this and each village having a primary agriculture society, by another 2 lakh
- FPOs/FPCs: Close to 18,000 (2023) its growing
- Agricultural Technology and Services: Entrepreneurs can develop and provide innovative agricultural technologies, tools, and services that improve productivity, reduce costs, and enhance the overall efficiency of farming operations. This can include precision farming solutions, farm management software, agricultural machinery and equipment, and access to modern irrigation systems. By offering these solutions to farmer communities, entrepreneurs can help increase agricultural productivity and ultimately contribute to doubling farmer incomes.
- Value Chain Enhancement: Entrepreneurs can focus on strengthening and enhancing the agricultural value chain. This involves establishing efficient post-harvest management systems, storage facilities, processing units, and value-added product development. By adding value to agricultural produce and reducing post-harvest losses, entrepreneurs can help farmers fetch better prices for their products, thereby increasing their incomes.
- Market Linkages and Access: Entrepreneurs can facilitate market linkages for farmers by establishing direct connections between farmers and consumers, retailers, exporters, and other stakeholders. This can involve setting up farmer cooperatives, online platforms, and distribution networks that ensure fair prices, reduce middlemen, and enable farmers to access wider markets. By bridging the gap between farmers and buyers, entrepreneurs can help farmers secure better market opportunities and improve their income potential.
- Financial Inclusion and Access to Credit. This can

include microfinance, crop insurance, and credit solutions that help farmers access timely and affordable credit. By facilitating financial inclusion, entrepreneurs can empower farmers to invest in modern farming practices, purchase high-quality inputs, and enhance their overall productivity and profitability.

• Capacity Building and Skill Development: Entrepreneurs can contribute to doubling farmer incomes by offering training, capacity building, and skill development programs for farmers. These programs can focus on sustainable farming practices, advanced agricultural techniques, market intelligence, and entrepreneurship skills. By equipping farmers with the necessary knowledge and skills, entrepreneurs can enhance their income-generating capabilities and foster a culture of innovation and entrepreneurship within the farming community.

• The agenda of doubling farmer income presents a vast range of opportunities for entrepreneurs to support farmer communities and farmer organizations. By leveraging innovative solutions, market linkages, financial inclusion, and capacity building, entrepreneurs can play a pivotal role in empowering farmers, improving agricultural productivity, and achieving the goal of doubling farmer incomes.

Case of HUM SHILPAKAR: facilitating ecommerce platforms for artisans and handicrafts sector

Case of HUM Shilpakar: Social Media based digital market for Artisan Entrepreneurs:

In response to the need for providing digital identity and market access to the Indian artisan community, an initiative called "HAM SHILPAKAR" was established. HAM SHILPAKAR is a social media-based platform specifically designed to help artisans connect with potential buyers and find markets for their unique products.

The Indian handloom and handicraft sector, known for its labor-intensive production methods, encompasses a wide range of high-value products such as Indian silk dresses, pottery, and handmade items crafted by talented artists and artisans. Unfortunately, over time, the manufacturers of these products have been facing challenges, leading to the disappearance of their unique creations.

Recognizing the importance of preserving and promoting these environmentally friendly, green products, HAM Shilpakar network, also known as the Artisans Network, conducted a comprehensive study. The study revealed the alarming decline in the number of manufacturers and the gradual disappearance of thousands of unique Indian products from the market.

To address this issue, HAM Shilpakar network has taken the initiative to provide a digital identity for manufacturers, cottage-based activities, potters, weavers, and handicraftsmen. By creating a dedicated platform, artisans can showcase their products, connect with potential buyers, and gain wider market access beyond their villages or panchayats.

The HAM Shilpakar platform serves as a bridge between artisans and buyers, enabling them to discover and engage with a diverse range of Indian handicrafts and handmade products. Through social media tools and features, artisans can share their stories, highlight their unique skills, and attract the attention of buyers who appreciate the beauty and craftsmanship of these products.

By leveraging technology and social media platforms, HAM Shilpakar network aims to revive the market presence of Indian artisans and their distinctive creations. The initiative not only promotes economic empowerment for artisans but also fosters the preservation of traditional craftsmanship, cultural heritage, and environmentally friendly practices.

In summary, the HAM SHILPAKAR initiative, conducted by the Artisans Network, focuses on providing a digital identity and market access for Indian artisans. By utilizing a social media-based platform, this initiative aims to revive the disappearing manufacturers and their unique, environmentally friendly products, fostering economic empowerment and preserving the rich cultural heritage of India's artisan community.

List of business ideas and entrepreneurial for youth:

1.   E-commerce platforms that focus on artisan products
2.   Support rural agro-businesses, farming community in terms of technology adoption:
3.   Set up agro-tech-smart farming companies
4.   Rural Green Entergy services like: Solar installation and maintance
5.   Exporting these products
6.   Facilitating exports
7.   Helping farmers, Small industrial, cottage industries, artisans set up E-Commerce stores and sell online on various platforms
8.   Digital marketing, brand building, social media presence
9.   Provide business support services of various kinds such business registration, Tax and compliance services; Information-Market data, market research
10.   Finacnial sector services for SMEs, Farming sector: Finance facilitation: arranging loans, insurance etc (crop insurance)

Project Progress Challenge: Elevate Your Entreprenuria Skills

1.	In what ways can you intervene or take action within these contexts?

2.	Could you explore the possibility of establishing a business that provides services to SMEs or farmers?

3.	Please identify farmers who are in need of fair prices for their products?

4.	what strategies can you employ to address this issue and develop a viable business model?

5.	Are there any specific handicrafts or traditional artisan businesses that are currently facing the threat of extinction?

6.	If so, how can you identify them and what measures can be taken to support and preserve them?

7.	Can you formulate a business plan that focuses on revitalizing these businesses and promoting their products in the global market?

8.	Work out a plan to facilitate export products of SMEs or Farmers?

9.	Prepare a business plan in an area of your choice?

References

Longenecker, J. G., Petty, J. W., Palich, L. E., & Hoy, F. (2022). Small Business Management: Launching & Growing Entrepreneurial Ventures - Softcover. Cengage Learning.
• Ries, E. (Year of publication not specified). The Lean Startup: How Today's Entrepreneurs Use Continuous Innovation to Create Radically Successful Businesses.
• World Bank. (Year not specified). Doing Business reports.
• Economist Intelligence Unit. (Year not specified). Economist's Business Environment Ranking.
• United Nations. (Year not specified). Reports on the Sustainable Development Goals (SDGs).
• Government of India. (Year not specified). Official publications on agriculture and economic reforms.
• United Nations, Department of Economic and Social Affairs. (Year not specified). Micro-, Small and Medium-sized Enterprises (MSMEs) and their role in achieving the Sustainable Development Goals.
• Koshy, P. (Year not specified). India's entrepreneurship policy: Future tasks and vision.
• Ministry of Micro, Small, and Medium Enterprises (Year not specified). Annual Reports.
• Institute for Social and Economic Change (ISED). (2022). India Micro Small and Medium Enterprises Report.

Unlocking Farmer Prosperity: Strategies for Multiplying Income and Strengthening Market Linkages

P Koshy

Enhancing the income of farmer households is crucial for improving their living standards, welfare, providing quality education for their children, reduce agrarian distress and bring parity between income of farmers and those working in non-agricultural professions. A significant growth in farmer income is crucial for #Indian #farmers, given the detrimental effects of low and fluctuating farm income. To address these challenges, governments have taken various measures. One notable strategy receiving attention is the agenda of doubling farmer income #DFI. The Inter-Ministerial Committee's recommendations focus on recognizing agriculture as a value-led enterprise(#NITI policy paper No.1/2017).

Given the possibilities and market potentials, tripling or quadrupling farmer income in the next couple of years, is not non-achievable or that ambitious a target. However, it is crucial to foster an agro-farmer friendly ecosystem. This ecosystem should prioritize involving farmers in decision-making processes, ensuring their active participation rather than relying solely on bureaucratic structures. The government's planned target to establish another two lakh Primary Agriculture societies, including dairy cooperative societies in every village is a game changer in this context.

Case of Leela: Grass fed desi ghee

Leela, a widow from #Kerala, shoulders the responsibility of caring for her family, which includes her three children, one is a college-going and other two unemployed due to disabilities. Together, they engage in organic farming, with a primary focus on dairy production. Leela's farming operation consists of 4 cows, including calves, and she relies on selling milk and dairy products as her main source of income.

Resourceful and mindful of local assets, Leela takes advantage of the abundant supply of grass found in nearby uncultivated paddy fields, in a central Travancore district of Kottayam, Kerala. This has allowed her to reduce her dependence on expensive cattle feed to a significant extent. Utilizing this locally available resource not only lowers her feed costs but also contributes to the unique qualities of her milk and dairy products. The organic ghee that Leela sells to non-residential Indians (NRIs) known for its distinct taste and aroma. Completely grass-fed, Leela's small farm is organic. Milk possesses exceptional quality, health benefits, and a delightful flavour. Unfortunately, Leela is not aware of the special qualities of #Grass-fed #cow's ghee that she sells. Organic grass fed-cow ghee market price on platforms like "#AmazonIndia" & #Flipakart, though varies, approximately INR 950 to INR 1000 for 500 grams, the local price remains at a significantly lower rate of INR 300 for the same quantity.

Despite her commitment to #organic farming and her diligent efforts in sourcing grass from #pesticide- and #fertilizer-free paddy fields, Leela faces challenges in obtaining fair prices for her products and accessing markets.

Addressing these issues and empowering farmers like Leela requires a comprehensive approach that includes raising awareness about the value and quality of their products, providing #market #access and marketing support, and equipping them with the knowledge and skills necessary to navigate the #digital #marketplace. By doing so, India can unlock the potential of its diverse agricultural products, empower small-scale farmers, and enable them to realize fair prices for their goods, ultimately contributing to the overall growth and development of the agricultural sector. This will help them enhance their income several times. Beyond doubling farmer income, it will result in.

Debabrata Mandal, a sr. consultant with EY India, who has been involved in facilitating the establishment and strengthening of farmer producer organizations/companies (#FPOs) highlights the crucial need to help farmers navigate the marketing process through e-ecommerce platforms and developing a pro-farm-er ecosystem, involving a collaborative approach involving all the stakeholders such as FPOs, cooperatives and host of other institutions and #NGOs. He says Indian farmers and agro-rural businesses offer a wide variety of unique products, but small and marginal farmers often lack awareness of the real market prices and the means to reaching out to the markets where consumers can afford to pay.

Cows and goats in agriculture economy: Farmer friendly institutions and dairy cooperatives

A noteworthy recommendation emerged during a discussion on agriculture sector in #Wayanad, #Malabar region-Kerala, organized by #TS Study Centre in conjunction with #Brahmagiri Development Society and #Ooralunkal Labour Society, held during the COVID-19 lockdown,– moderated by Prof. Dr Jose George (Rtd), #Mumbai University and Prof. Dr. R. Ramku-mar, TISS Mumbai, would be of relevance to revisit. This was related to the role of primary dairy cooperative societies. The suggestion called for transforming primary dairy societies at the village level into hubs for farmer-agriculture services, where the government can reach out to farmers with their services. Ac-cording to the proponent of this idea, such an approach would not only simplify farmers' lives but also ensure that services effectively reach the real farmers. Making primary dairy societies central hubs for farmer-agriculture services. This would not only benefit farmers but also facilitate the government in efficiently delivering its services to the agricultural community. Making services available at a centralized location, adjacent to dairy farmer societies where they mostly congregate for various purposes may help farmers have easy access to services and a centralized space for marketing their produce, improving efficiency and convenience.

Farmer-Friendly Agriculture Support Ecosystem
By recognizing the importance of dairy cooperatives and promoting their collaboration with agriculture departments, India can harness the potential of these cooperatives to uplift farmers and enhance agricultural development.

In India, cows and goats play a central role in the farming activities, providing farmers with a regular source of income. Alongside poultry farming, whether on a small or medium scale, cow and goat farming proves to be lucrative. It is worth noting that India holds the distinction of being the largest milk producer globally, contributing a significant 23% share to the total global milk production.

Critical importance of village level primary dairy cooperatives has to emerge at the centre of farmer friendly eco-system. Unfortunately, the connection between dairy cooperatives and farmers is often overlooked. It is crucial to establish a collaborative strategy between agriculture departments and dairy cooperatives, considering the significant role of them in our economy. There are more than thirty state dairy cooperatives with a close around one lakh ninety thousand (199,182) primary dairy cooperative societies with around 1.5 crore members, are engaged in procurement of milk from the farmers, providing milk testing facilities, cattle feed sale, extension services, etc. to the members. Farmers frequently visit these primary dairy societies, making them the primary point of contact for farmers. In fact, farmers tend to have deeper dependence and interaction with these societies compared to the government's agriculture departments.

Reaching out to farmers: case of Goat Trust

The Goat Trust, an organization implementing innovative initiatives in livestock farming, has highlighted the importance of reaching out to farmers. It emphasizes that relying solely on a bureaucratic approach is insufficient to support the agriculture and farming sectors or create more job opportunities.
The Goat Trust focus on addressing farmer challenges within various sub-sectors by providing training to locally available farmers. For instance, #PashuSakhi (#LivestockNurse) initiative, focuses on training semi-literate or illiterate women in structured classrooms and field practices. This program equips them with basic knowledge on improved livestock practices, preventative care, and herb-based home remedies at a low cost. As goat rearers themselves, these trained women actively disseminate their knowledge and skills within their villages, leading to improved livestock management, reduced mortality and morbidity rates, and overall better outcomes.

Community Livestock Manager program targets rural youth, both men and women, engaged in livestock farming. Through this program, they receive training to support Pashu Sakhis and establish linkages for input and output services. These individuals can then become livestock business entrepreneurs and service providers, eventually managing livestock business centers on a cost-recovery basis. This program empowers the youth to grow their businesses and contribute to the overall development of the livestock sector.

Strategies to multiply farmer income

Debabrata Mondal identifies following approach to effectively increase farmer income. Those key strategies include, "implementing collective marketing initiatives, reducing input costs through fertilizer subsidies, facilitating exports, establishing minimum support prices and government procurement mechanisms, fostering linkages with exporters, promoting crop cultivation based on market demand, and encouraging organic cultivation and branding". Its also important to shift to smart farming, as the way technology-intensive modern farms function. Smart farming is critical for making farming more sustainable and profitable. "Without high tech , the farmer breed will become extinct soon. And That's the only way farming can be made profitable, says Akhil, team leader at Agro-tech solutions, a Kerala based agro-tech solutions company.

To conclude, by implementing these strategies and leveraging the efforts of NGOs and other stakeholders, India can make significant progress towards doubling farmer income, uplifting rural livelihoods, and ensuring sustainable agricultural development. The successful implementation of these recommendations requires a comprehensive approach that includes policy support, infrastructure development, access to credit and technology, and capacity building for farmers. By holistically addressing these factors, India can achieve sustainable and significant improvements in farmers' income levels.

Source:
P. Koshy, Global SME News, 4 July 2023, https://globalsmenews.com/unlocking-farmer-prosperity-strategies-for-multiplying-income-and-strengthening-market-linkages/

Khadi: the new corporate attire?

Emerging global order and #BRICS: a new world that welcomes indegenous traditions, a move away from single global culture
Khadi's Unique Blend of Tradition and Sustainability: Discover how adopting Khadi as corporate attire not only showcases a commitment to Indian culture but also supports eco-friendly practices, preserving traditional craftsmanship and empowering local communities. Unlock the potential of sustainable fashion and responsible consumption with Khadi's versatile and timeless appeal.

Why should Khadi and traditional Indian fashion be the preferred corporate attire? Beyond yoga, meditation and Indian spiritual values to Indian traditional attire adoption at corporate level will help promote and globalize Indian products. Khadar-Khadi made dresses as formal dress code for Indian corporates will be promoting not just weavers and cottage industries but also help instil a sense of national pride among employees and demonstrates a deep connection to Indian culture and traditions.

In a world where the challenges of climate change loom large, it is essential that responsible manufacturing and consumption are reflected at every level. Its time to adopt green practices at all levels. From saving on office stationery, adopting to more sustainable office stationery products, energy saving and avoiding power wastage and energy efficient building designs to so many other aspects. Here, formal dress codes that are attuned to local culture, traditions, climatic realities are also part of sustainability. Particularly by adopting a dress code which includes Khadi-Kha-

dar made fabrics and Khadi-KVIC products, corporates will be contributing to sustainable development goals:
#SDG8 ;#SDG12.

Khadi: Economic Growth, Responsible production & Consumption

The Indian corporate world must shift to adopting traditional attire and fashion trends too in their formal dress code menu. Khadi-Khadar fibre made dresses provide greater comfort both during the summer and winter and keep body temperature regulated and make one fresh throughout the day. Sustainable Development Goal (SDG 12) focuses on Responsible Consumption and Production of Khadi and traditional Indian fashion offer a compelling case as the preferred corporate attire, especially in a world striving to combat climate change. By embracing this sustainable and culturally rich choice, companies can align themselves with responsible practices, contribute to the preservation of traditional craftsmanship, and create a positive impact on both their workforce and the environment.

Emerging global order and #BRICS: a new world that welcomes indegenous traditions, a move away from single global culture India with an ancient civilization, entrepreneurial culture and legacy, its private sector too need to showcase its unique traditions in private corporate dress code. With BRICS emerging as an economic gravitational force in the emerging world, India has a significant position in the world of business. Its huge market attracts corporates, brands and businesses from world over, which is an opportunity for Khadi, weavers, artisans and cottage industries, which all stand apart for its green processes, technologies and sustainability approaches. Global culture with significant space for local cultures, swadeshi dress and fashion trends as both formal and casual corporate dress code. This has many benefits for the corporates as well.

In an era where environmental consciousness and sustainable practices are gaining momentum, introducing Khadi-Handmade clothing as a new corporate dress code can unlock a plethora of positive impacts. With a strong focus on incorporating eco-friendly practices into the corporate world, companies have the unique opportunity to reduce their ecological footprint while supporting local communities and artisans

Consuming products from sectors that create more jobs, livelihoods, more families and thereby contributing to reduce poverty. Shifting to Khadi or products from village industries that use more labour intensive techniques will contribute in raising sustainability of micro and cottage enterprises. Can the corporate executives adopt Khadi cotton made suits and dresses? If the large scale industry, corporate world and the government employees massively adopt Khadi and micro-cottage industry products as part of their life, overall economic development in India will emerge more sustainable.

Charkka represents economic freedom & financial independence, self-sufficiency and the vibrant entrepreneurial culture of India. Growing acceptance and demand for hand made products particularly khadi clothes represent changing fashion trends. Freedom from Robots, machines and carbon emission Traditional cottage manufacturing, which is labour intensive are often sustainable. They come out from a responsible manufacturing process. Chakka- Khadi products, labour intensive in nature, promotes sustainable practices. While they are oriented to green technologies, manufacturing process they are the solution for a world which is troubled by carbon emission, human replacing technologies and climate change challenges. The product offerings are healthy, green and contributes to job creation, regional economic development and supports entrepreneurs of micro and tiny sector. Clothes created by Khadi and weavers of handloom sector are not only   comfortable but are becoming fashion trend of today.

Khadi as corporate dress code: advantages

Introducing Khadi-Handmade clothes as a new corporate dress code can have several positive impacts. The Indian hand-woven textile industry, specifically Khadi, is known for its sustainable and eco-friendly practices. Here are some reasons why it could be beneficial to adopt Khadi-Handmade clothes as a corporate dress code:

Environmental Sustainability: Khadi is made from natural fibers such as cotton, silk, and wool, which are biodegradable and have a lower environmental impact compared to synthetic materials. By promoting Khadi as the dress code, companies can contribute to reducing their carbon footprint and supporting sustainable fashion.
Preservation of Traditional Crafts: Encouraging the use of Khadi promotes traditional Indian crafts and helps sustain the livelihoods of artisans involved in hand weaving. This supports rural economies and preserves the rich cultural heritage of India.
Social Responsibility: Adopting Khadi-Handmade clothes as a dress code aligns with corporate social responsibility initiatives. It showcases a commitment to promoting ethical and sustainable practices and can enhance a company's reputation in the eyes of customers, employees, and stakeholders.

Employee Well-being: Khadi fabric is known for its comfort and breathability, making it suitable for daily wear. Employees would appreciate the comfort and natural feel of these clothes, which can contribute to their overall well-being and productivity.
Unique Identity: Embracing Khadi as the corporate dress code can give an organization a distinct identity. It reflects a commitment to Indian culture and heritage, setting the company apart

from others and fostering a sense of pride among employees.
No alt text provided for this image

Khadi (KVIC) gaining new heights

In the recent years, thanks to enhanced promotional effort, government push as well shifting fashion trends and taste for cotton & hand made products globally, Khadi and Village Industries Commission (KVIC) has achieved a massive turnover of Rs 1.15 lakh crore, from 2014-15, the production in the Khadi sector in 2021-22 has increased by 191%, while the Khadi sales have increased exponentially by 332%, which also resulting better pay & compensation , monthly income of artisans by around 33% and 10 % hike in the wages of weavers. The sector (Khadi & Village Industries Commission) engages five lakh people directly and indirectly many more (MSME, Annual Report 2022-23,P.54) However, it is important to consider practical aspects such as availability, affordability, and individual preferences. Not everyone may find Khadi clothing accessible or affordable.

To conclude, Khadi will take Indian corporate sector much greater heights.

Khadi is not just a fabric; it represents a significant chapter in India's history, symbolizing the spirit of self-reliance and freedom. Images of Mahatma Gandhi spinning a charkha and Khadi products generate feelings of national pride and the need for self-reliance among Indians. The integration of Khadi as corporate attire will not only foster a profound connection to Indian culture and traditions but also induce a strong sense of national pride among employees.

Source: P. Koshy, "Khadi: the new corporate attire?", Global SME News, 25 July 2023, https://globalsmenews.com/khadi-the-new-corporate-attire/

www.ingramcontent.com/pod-product-compliance
Lightning Source LLC
Chambersburg PA
CBHW060854260726
48661CB00008B/3259